Crawford

by Iain Gray

LangSyne
PUBLISHING
WRITING *to* REMEMBER

79 Main Street, Newtongrange,
Midlothian EH22 4NA
Tel: 0131 344 0414 Fax: 0845 075 6085
E-mail: info@lang-syne.co.uk
www.langsyneshop.co.uk

Design by Dorothy Meikle
Printed by Ricoh Print Scotland

ISBN 978-1-85217-109-4

Crawford

Crawford

MOTTO:
I will give you safety by strength.

CREST:
A stag's head with a cross between the antlers.

TERRITORY:
Lanarkshire, Ayrshire, Renfrewshire.

Chapter one:

The origins of the clan system

by Rennie McOwan

The original Scottish clans of the Highlands and the great families of the Lowlands and Borders were gatherings of families, relatives, allies and neighbours for mutual protection against rivals or invaders.

Scotland experienced invasion from the Vikings, the Romans and English armies from the south. The Norman invasion of what is now England also had an influence on land-holding in Scotland. Some of these invaders stayed on and in time became 'Scottish'.

The word clan derives from the Gaelic language term 'clann', meaning children, and it was first used many centuries ago as communities were formed around tribal lands in glens and mountain fastnesses.

The format of clans changed over the centuries, but at its best the chief and his family held the land on behalf of all, like trustees, and the ordinary clansmen and women believed they had a blood relationship with the founder of their clan.

There were two way duties and obligations. An inadequate chief could be deposed and replaced by someone of greater ability.

Clan people had an immense pride in race. Their relationship with the chief was like adult children to a father and they had a real dignity.

The concept of clanship is very old and a more feudal notion of authority gradually crept in.

Pictland, for instance, was divided into seven principalities ruled by feudal leaders who were the strongest and most charismatic leaders of their particular groups.

By the sixth century the 'British' kingdoms of Strathclyde, Lothian and Celtic Dalriada (Argyll) had emerged and Scotland, as one nation, began to take shape in the time of King Kenneth MacAlpin.

Some chiefs claimed descent from

ancient kings which may not have been accurate in every case.

By the twelfth and thirteenth centuries the clans and families were more strongly brought under the central control of Scottish monarchs.

Lands were awarded and administered more and more under royal favour, yet the power of the area clan chiefs was still very great.

The long wars to ensure Scotland's independence against the expansionist ideas of English monarchs extended the influence of some clans and reduced the lands of others.

Those who supported Scotland's greatest king, Robert the Bruce, were awarded the territories of the families who had opposed his claim to the Scottish throne.

In the Scottish Borders country – the notorious Debatable Lands – the great families built up a ferocious reputation for providing warlike men accustomed to raiding into England and occasionally fighting one another.

Chiefs had the power to dispense justice and to confiscate lands and clan warfare produced a society where martial virtues – courage, hardiness, tenacity – were greatly admired.

Gradually the relationship between the clans and the Crown became strained as Scottish monarchs became more orientated to life in the Lowlands and, on occasion, towards England.

The Highland clans spoke a different language, Gaelic, whereas the language of Lowland Scotland and the court was Scots and in more modern times, English.

Highlanders dressed differently, had different customs, and their wild mountain land sometimes seemed almost foreign to people living in the Lowlands.

It must be emphasised that Gaelic culture was very rich and story-telling, poetry, piping, the clarsach (harp) and other music all flourished and were greatly respected.

Highland culture was different from other parts of Scotland but it was not inferior or less sophisticated.

Central Government, whether in London or Edinburgh, sometimes saw the Gaelic clans as

"The spirit of the clan means much to thousands of people"

a challenge to their authority and some sent expeditions into the Highlands and west to crush the power of the Lords of the Isles.

Nevertheless, when the eighteenth century Jacobite Risings came along the cause of the Stuarts was mainly supported by Highland clans.

The word Jacobite comes from the Latin for James – Jacobus. The Jacobites wanted to restore the exiled Stuarts to the throne of Britain.

The monarchies of Scotland and England became one in 1603 when King James VI of Scotland (1st of England) gained the English throne after Queen Elizabeth died.

The Union of Parliaments of Scotland and England, the Treaty of Union, took place in 1707.

Some Highland clans, of course, and Lowland families opposed the Jacobites and supported the incoming Hanoverians.

After the Jacobite cause finally went down at Culloden in 1746 a kind of ethnic cleansing took place. The power of the chiefs was curtailed. Tartan and the pipes were banned in law.

Many emigrated, some because they

wanted to, some because they were evicted by force. In addition, many Highlanders left for the cities of the south to seek work.

Many of the clan lands became home to sheep and deer shooting estates.

But the warlike traditions of the clans and the great Lowland and Border families lived on, with their descendants fighting bravely for freedom in two world wars.

Remember the men from whence you came, says the Gaelic proverb, and to that could be added the role of many heroic women.

The spirit of the clan, of having roots, whether Highland or Lowland, means much to thousands of people.

Chapter two:

In freedom's cause

One of the great Lowland families, the Crawfords have played a key role at pivotal points in Scotland's long and colourful story.

In common with many families and clans their origins are shrouded in the mists of obscurity, but a gleam of light is discernible when we learn that, following the Battle of Hastings in 1066, an Anglo-Danish chief known as Thorlongus, or Thor the Tall, found refuge in Berwickshire.

Thorlongus was a descendant of Viking raiders who had settled centuries earlier on the east coast of England, intermarried with the Anglo-Saxons already settled there, and rose to the ranks of the nobility.

Following his invasion of England in 1066 the Norman Conqueror, William, launched a campaign of persecution against nobles such as Thorlongus, and many fled their lands and estates for both sanctuary and a new life in Scotland.

At some stage between 1097 and 1107, Thorlongus was granted lands at Ednam, near Kelso, in the Borders, by King Edgar.

His son, Swane, had a son known as Galfridus Swaneson, who settled in Lanarkshire and was later granted the Barony of Crawford, in Upper Clydesdale, between 1105 and 1110.

It is from the land, or territory, known as Crawford, also spelled Craufurd, that the former Anglo-Danes took the name by which they would gain fame in the succeeding centuries.

There are three possible origins for the name 'Crawford'. One is that it comes from 'craw', or 'crow', and 'ford', or 'furd', meaning a river crossing, while another is that it indicates a cattle crossing.

The more likely explanation is that it stems from 'cru-furd', or 'cru-ford', with 'cru' indicating 'bloody', hence 'bloody ford' or 'bloody crossing' – because it is known that the area was witness to a number of savage battles, particularly between invading Roman legions and local tribes.

The first official reference to the Crawford name in Scottish records occurs in 1127, during the reign of King David I, when the two brothers Sir John and Sir Gregan Crawford are recorded as among the Scottish knights serving the monarch.

It was Sir John, who died in 1140, who gave his name to the Lanarkshire village of Crawfordjohn, while his brother, Gregan, gained eternal fame for his family after saving the life of his king in 1127.

King David, according to legend, had been hunting in the grounds of what would later become the abbey and palace of Holyrood, in Edinburgh, when Sir Gregan Crawford saved him from a charging stag.

A grateful king, the legend runs, rewarded his loyal knight by granting him lands in Ayrshire, and later founded the Holy Cross (Holyrood) Abbey in thanks for his salvation.

The incident is commemorated in the Crawford crest of a stag with a cross between its antlers, and the family motto of 'I will give you safety by strength.'

The Crawford power and influence increased dramatically in 1196 when William the Lyon appointed Sir Reginald Crawford of Crawfordjohn to the powerful post of hereditary Sheriff of Ayr, on Scotland's west coast.

Just over 300 years later, in 1499, the family had established the three main branches that are recognised today. These are the Crawfords of Auchinames, in Renfrewshire, the Craufurds of Craufurdland, near Kilmarnock, in Ayrshire, and the Crawfords of Kilbirnie, also in Ayrshire.

The head of the family, by tradition, is recognised as belonging to the Auchinames branch, which traces its descent from the original Crawford sheriffs of Ayr.

The last registered head of the family, however, Hugh Crawford, sold off all his heritable property before his death in Alberta, Canada, in the 1960s.

Although some Crawfords recognise a close family link with the renowned Lindsay clan – through the marriage in the 12th century of a

Crawford woman to David Lindsay, ancestor of the Earls of Crawford and Balcarres – the Crawford family is officially recognised as a distinct family, with its own proud heritage and tradition and not, as some argue, a sept, or branch, of the Lindsays.

A more significant marriage made in the 12th century was that of Margaret Crawford, a sister of the then Sheriff of Ayr, to Sir Malcolm Wallace.

This resulted in Margaret Crawford becoming the mother of the great Scottish hero and patriot William Wallace, a connection with which the Crawfords can be justly proud.

Controversy exists to this day over whether Wallace was born on his father's lands of Elderslie, near Paisley, or if these lands were actually the lands of Ellerslie, near Kilmarnock.

In the wider scheme of the great Wars of Independence, however, the location of Wallace's birth in about 1272 is unimportant. He raised the banner of revolt against the English occupation of Scotland in May of 1297, after slaying Sir William Heselrig, Sheriff of Lanark, in revenge for the killing of his young wife, Marion.

Proving an expert in the tactics of guerrilla warfare, Wallace and his hardened band of freedom fighters inflicted stunning defeats on the English garrisons.

This culminated in the liberation of practically all of Scotland following the battle of Stirling Bridge, on September 11, 1297.

Defeated at the battle of Falkirk on July 22, 1298, after earlier being appointed Guard-ian of Scotland, Sir William Wallace was eventually betrayed and captured in August of 1305, and, on the black day for Scotland of August 23 of that year, he was brutally executed in London on the orders of a vengeful Edward I of England, better known as The Hammer of the Scots.

Wallace's Crawford relations also paid dearly for their support of the great patriot.

His uncle, Sir Reginald Crawford, was executed at Carlisle in 1303, while his grandfather on his mother's side, Sir Hugh Crawford, was treacherously murdered after he and other prominent landholders were lured to Ayr under what they believed was an English guarantee of safe conduct and unceremoniously hanged.

Wallace later gained vengeance for the action by slaughtering the English garrison at Ayr.

A cousin of Wallace, Sir William Crawford of Elcho, accompanied him to the French court in 1299 to seek support for the cause of Scotland's freedom.

Crawfords also fought for the cause of the great warrior king Robert the Bruce at the battle of Bannockburn, in 1314, and it was as reward for their service that Bruce granted them the lands of Auchinames.

Robert III in 1391 confirmed the lands of Craufurd of Craufurdland, while the Kilbirnie estates were acquired one hundred years later, in 1499.

Chapter three:

Commandos and ministers

A strong martial spirit continued to run throughout the succeeding centuries through the bloodstream of the Crawfords, with Sir William Craufurd of Craufurdland, for example, being recognised during the reign of James I as one of the bravest men of his times.

Along with other Scots with a taste for foreign adventure and a good battle, he fought in the service of the French monarch against the English and was wounded in 1423 at the siege of Creyult, in Burgundy.

Two senior members of branches of the Crawford family, John Craufurd of Craufurdland and the Laird of Auchinames, fell with their king, James IV, at the disastrous battle of Flodden on September 9, 1513.

They were among 5,000 Scots, including

two bishops, 11 earls, 15 barons, and 300 knights, who were slain by a more tactically astute English force led by Thomas Howard, Earl of Surrey.

Nearly 34 years later to the day, on September 10, 1547, the military commander Captain Thomas Crawford of Jordanhill was among the Scots captured and imprisoned for a time in England following defeat at the battle of Pinkie, near Musselburgh.

The battle was fought during the period known as the Rough Wooing, when England's Henry VIII sought at the point of a sword to persuade the Scots to agree to a proposal for the marriage of the infant Mary, Queen of Scots, to his son, Edward.

Archibald Crawford, a Lord of Session and secretary to Mary's mother, Queen Mary of Guise, accompanied her body in 1560 from Scotland to Rheims, in France, for burial.

By 1571, Mary, Queen of Scots was being held in confinement in England following her flight there after defeat at the battle of Langside, near Glasgow, three years earlier.

The strategically important bastion of Dumbarton Castle, atop Dumbarton Rock in the Firth of Clyde, however, was still held by her supporters, and it was vital that her enemies seize it in order to prevent a French fleet from reinforcing it from the Irish Sea or disembarking an army on the mainland.

Captain Thomas Crawford of Jordanhill, none the worse from his imprisonment in England following the battle of Pinkie 24 years earlier, was chosen to lead an intrepid band of 150 men for what seemed an almost impossible task.

In the 16th century equivalent of a commando raid, and in the late hours of a misty April night, Crawford and his band assembled at the foot of the towering basaltic rock equipped with ladders with attached iron clamps and lengths of stout rope.

With Crawford leading the way, they began their hair-raising and tortuous ascent of what was considered the most inaccessible section of the rock, the area from which the defenders would least expect an attack.

Spotted by a lone sentry just after clambering over the castle battlements, Crawford and his band swiftly turned and trained the castle's own cannon onto the rudely awoken garrison.

Crawford's daring assault had worked, and before the sun had risen he and his men had taken the supposedly impregnable fortress with only four fatalities – all on the side of the defenders.

In addition to his allegiance to his own family of Crawford, Captain Crawford was also a kinsman of the Earl of Lennox, father of Lord Darnley, Mary's murdered husband, and he is also remembered for the key role he played in what is known as the Casket Letters controversy.

The letters involved alleged correspondence between Mary and Bothwell that implicated her in the conspiracy to murder her husband. Evidence from Crawford apparently vouched for the authenticity of the incriminating letters.

Captain Crawford is buried in Kilbirnie churchyard, in Ayrshire, and his recumbent figure fittingly shows the veteran military commander clad in full armour.

In common with his distinguished relation Captain Thomas Crawford, Lawrence Crawford, born in 1611, was a staunch Presbyterian. It was in defence of the Protestant cause that he fought on the Continent for the Swedish king Gustavus Adolphus during the bitter Thirty Years War.

Returning later to fight on the Parliamentary side against Charles I, he was killed in 1645 at the siege of Hereford.

He must have had something of a rather fearless and irascible temperament, for he is known to have frequently quarrelled with the great Lord Protector himself, Oliver Cromwell!

Another staunch defender of the Presbyterian faith was Hugh Crawford, the younger son of the laird of Auchinames, who was appointed the first minister at New Cumnock, in his native Ayrshire, in 1653, during the sorrowful time of bloody struggle between the opposing forces of the Crown and the Presbyterian Covenanters.

Described as having been 'one of Ayrshire's band of true covenanting ministers',

Hugh Crawford literally took to the hills to preach at open-air conventicles after being expelled from his parish.

He was banished from Scotland in May of 1683 and found refuge in Ireland, returning to his homeland after the 'Glorious Revolution' of 1688 when William of Orange was invited to take over the united thrones of Scotland and England.

Chapter four:

Washer of the Sovereign's Hands

The 20th Laird of Craufurdland, John Walkinshaw Craufurd, distinguished himself not only as a great soldier but also for an act of friendship that effectively scuppered his further promotion prospects within the army.

An adherent of the Hanoverian cause, he had fought on the side of the detested Duke of Cumberland at the battle of Culloden in April of 1746, after which a number of captured Jacobites were sentenced to execution.

Among them was the Earl of Kilmarnock who, although on the opposing side to Craufurd, was still his friend.

Craufurd, who had fought with distinction at both the battles of Dettingen and Fontenoy, found his name was put to the bottom of the Army List as punishment for his charitable action in retrieving the Earl's severed head after his execution on London's Tower Hill and arranging for his remains to receive decent Christian burial.

After his death in 1793 his astonished family learned that for some inexplicable reason he had left his entire estates to the wealthy banker Sir Thomas Coutts.

The will was contested, however, and the case finally resolved in 1806 in favour of the family.

It was during the reign of James V (1513-1542), that a bizarre incident occurred that resulted in the Laird of Craufurdland to this day being distinguished with the rather odd ceremonial title of Washer of the Sovereign's Hands.

James V, when the fancy frequently took him, would travel the countryside incognito, in the guise of 'The Gude Man of Ballengeich.'

On one such excursion, the monarch was attacked by a band of robbers at Cramond Bridge, near Edinburgh. A doughty farmer by the name of Jock Houison, who farmed the king's own land of nearby Braehead, came to the rescue.

Jock managed to fight off the robbers and

took 'the gude man' back to his humble farmhouse, where he carefully washed and tended his wounds.

Unaware he was actually addressing his king, Jock informed him that it was his great ambition to one day own his own farm.

Thanking him for washing his wounds, the 'gude man' urged Jock to visit him soon 'at the castle'. Mystified why 'the gude man' should be found at Edinburgh Castle, Jock nevertheless set off later to find him.

One can only imagine the farmer's astonishment when it was revealed that the bedraggled stranger whose wounds he had tended was actually the king.

A further surprise was in store for Jock when the king gifted his farm to him and his descendants as a token of thanks.

There was one important condition attached, however. This requires that once during the reign of every monarch the three eldest male descendants of Jock Houison should ceremoniously wash the monarch's hands.

In order of age, they are required to hold

the basin, ewer, and silver salver with linen towel – hence the title of Washer of the Sovereign's Hands.

Through the marriage in 1744 between Elizabeth Craufurd of Craufurdland and John Houison of Braehead, the Craufurds of Craufurdland are now known as the Houison Craufurds.

Peter Houison Craufurd, the present laird of Craufurdland and Braehead, and whose family lives in Craufurdland Castle, near Kilmarnock, has performed the ceremony on three occasions – for Edward VIII, George VI, and Queen Elizabeth II.

Crawfords have also gained fame on the international stage, quite literally in the case of the British actor Michael Crawford and the late Hollywood screen idols Joan Crawford and Broderick Crawford, while supermodel Cindy Crawford has achieved celebrity on the international catwalk.

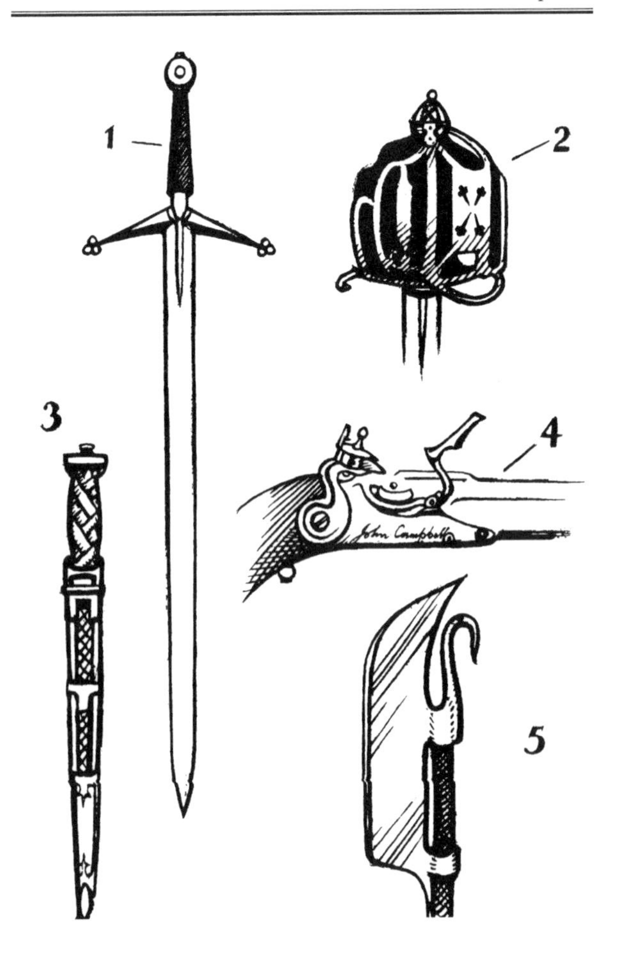
1
2
3
4
John Campbell
5

Clan weapons

1) The claymore or two-handed sword
(fifteenth or early sixteenth century)

2) Basket hilt of broadsword
made in Stirling, 1716

3) Highland dirk
(eighteenth century)

4) Steel pistol *(detail)* made in Doune

5) Head of Lochaber Axe as carried
in the '45 and earlier